This Journal Belongs To:

_____

THE BLENDED FAMILY JOURNAL FOR STEPMOMS

Prompts and Practices for Navigating Change

Sonya Jensen, LMFT

ROCKRIDGE PRESS

Copyright © 2021 by Rockridge Press, Emeryville, California

No part of this publication may be reproduced, stored in a retrieval system, or transmitted in any form or by any means, electronic, mechanical, photocopying, recording, scanning, or otherwise, except as permitted under Sections 107 or 108 of the 1976 United States Copyright Act, without the prior written permission of the Publisher. Requests to the Publisher for permission should be addressed to the Permissions Department, Rockridge Press, 6005 Shellmound Street, Suite 175, Emeryville, CA 94608.

Limit of Liability/Disclaimer of Warranty: The Publisher and the author make no representations or warranties with respect to the accuracy or completeness of the contents of this work and specifically disclaim all warranties, including without limitation warranties of fitness for a particular purpose. No warranty may be created or extended by sales or promotional materials. The advice and strategies contained herein may not be suitable for every situation. This work is sold with the understanding that the Publisher is not engaged in rendering medical, legal, or other professional advice or services. If professional assistance is required, the services of a competent professional person should be sought. Neither the Publisher nor the author shall be liable for damages arising herefrom. The fact that an individual, organization, or website is referred to in this work as a citation and/or potential source of further information does not mean that the author or the Publisher endorses the information the individual, organization, or website may provide or recommendations they/it may make. Further, readers should be aware that websites listed in this work may have changed or disappeared between when this work was written and when it is read.

For general information on our other products and services or to obtain technical support, please contact our Customer Care Department within the United States at (866) 744-2665, or outside the United States at (510) 253-0500.

Rockridge Press publishes its books in a variety of electronic and print formats. Some content that appears in print may not be available in electronic books, and vice versa.

TRADEMARKS: Rockridge Press and the Rockridge Press logo are trademarks or registered trademarks of Callisto Media Inc. and/or its affiliates, in the United States and other countries, and may not be used without written permission. All other trademarks are the property of their respective owners. Rockridge Press is not associated with any product or vendor mentioned in this book.

Interior and Cover Designer: Marietta Anastassatos
Art Producer: Hannah Dickerson
Editor: Carolyn Abate
Production Editor: Ellina Litmanovich
Production Manager: Martin Worthington

All illustrations used under license from iStock.com and Shutterstock.com

Author photo courtesy of Anna Kraft

Paperback ISBN: 978-1-63807-904-0
R0

Contents

Introduction VII

SECTION 1: **EMBRACE WHO YOU ARE** 1

SECTION 2: **DEFINE YOUR NEW ROLE** 27

SECTION 3: **FOSTERING PATIENCE AND COMPASSION** 55

SECTION 4: **EVERYONE BENEFITS FROM BOUNDARIES** 83

SECTION 5: **NURTURE YOUR RELATIONSHIPS** 113

SECTION 6: **NAVIGATE THE ROAD AHEAD** 139

A Final Word 164

Resources 166

References 167

What we know matters, but who we are matters more.

—Brené Brown

Introduction

Welcome! Becoming a stepmom is truly a time of transition and change. Whether you are blending your family with your partner's or entering into a new family without kids of your own, this journal will help you navigate your new role without losing your identity.

There is no one way to be a stepmom. You may be more involved in your stepkids' lives, or you may even take on the role of primary mother figure to younger children. Maybe you're a stepmom to older children or children who aren't comfortable with this change yet. Whatever your situation, I'm so glad you are here.

Think of this journal as your place for encouragement and personal development. Here you will come to experience the vast range of emotions that come with transition. You will explore the depths of who you are, where you've come from, and where you're going. I know you want to do your best and have high hopes and expectations for yourself to be the best stepmom you can be.

As a licensed marriage and family therapist, I've worked with many people through the transition of blending their families and lives. My clients always begin this process with hope and try to carry themselves through the ups and downs, the heartbreaks and the triumphs, with that same hope. But it's hard to do alone—no one can. Why? Because change requires us to meet a new version of ourselves, to face our fears of the unknown. We need people cheering us on and a strong foundation with our partner that is balanced in both communication and emotional intimacy.

I've always had a natural desire for the people I meet not to feel alone. Everyone should find a community that supports and provides resources that make hard times feel a little lighter. This journal will help you connect more deeply to yourself, your partner, your children, and others around you. You will evaluate the things you desire, have, and don't have, and what it feels like to build a life you love with your partner and stepchildren, together, as a family.

The term "blended family" is the blending of two lives, involving children from one or both partners, moving from previous relationships into one. The act of commitment to another person can be complex, exhilarating, overwhelming, and scary. Add children into that mix, and those same feelings become amplified. Not only are you trying to navigate how you and your partner will manage your new routine and daily life, but now you have potential custody schedules, after-school sports and activities, and other complications to deal with.

When merging families, many couples and individuals try to figure out how to make time for themselves and each other while building a relationship with their "new" children. Together, we will create what I call "rituals of connection," which will help you make and sustain times of connection to yourself, your partner, and the kids, while still prioritizing your values. Often, people believe that you must give all your time to this new adventure, but what many don't realize is that it's not about quantity of time, but quality of time. I will show you how to build mindfulness and self-check-ins into your day-to-day experiences that connect to what truly matters to you.

Throughout this journal, I will introduce you to a variety of insightful prompts and exercises, as well as inspiring quotes and affirmations. Each section will give you an opportunity to discover what methods and techniques work best for you, and you will use your intuition and life experiences to take from it what you bring to your family. I encourage you to try every exercise and answer every prompt and see what comes to the surface. You may surprise yourself with the questions or activities that ground you and change your perspective.

Come to this journal regularly with an open mind and an open heart. You can complete these activities in order or use them in a way and time that works best for you! Remember, be gentle with yourself. Take your time working through this journal. No matter your pace, learn to trust in the timing of things and your intuition to guide you through this process.

This journal is a journey toward finding yourself, defining your new role as a stepmom, building patience and compassion, identifying and setting healthy boundaries, fostering connection, and building a plan for the future that is sustainable and inspiring. As a therapist specializing in couples work, I've seen amazing women struggle to find their balance, give themselves grace and compassion, and embrace who they are as a stepmom. It can be challenging to connect with the new children who are now a part of your life. No matter where you find yourself in this journey, this journal is for you!

I hope that, after reading this journal, you will feel inspired, refreshed, and ready to take on the new challenges you're facing (or going to face) as a new stepmom. However, this journal is not a substitute for therapy and/or medication to manage anxiety and depression. If you feel you need to, you can use this journal in conjunction with therapy as a tool to enrich the dialogue between you and your therapist and develop new goals in that process that match your needs. There is no shame in seeking support and finding a therapist who fits your communication style and preference. (See the Resources on page 167 for more information.)

This time is all for you—savor it and cherish the time you spend with yourself. Nobody handles any transition perfectly, but by showing up you are making the choice to be the best stepmom you can be. Show yourself grace. Give yourself permission to have some fun, shed some tears, and make lifelong, enriching connections with others. You're not alone on this journey, and every minute you spend investing in yourself is a minute well spent. Let's get started!

INTRODUCTION

Always be a first-rate version of yourself and not a second-rate version of someone else.

—Judy Garland

SECTION 1

EMBRACE WHO YOU ARE

We're all shaped and molded into the person we are today by our past relationships and experiences. Sometimes we fear who we are based on either our lack of experience or our mistakes; and sometimes we own who we are and know our strengths and weaknesses. Either way, to move forward and to push deeper, we must first understand where we came from. By doing this, we learn who we are and why we feel the way we do, and can make intentional choices for the future. This section includes prompts and exercises that will increase your awareness and connection to yourself and your past. It will help you pause and reflect on what makes you . . . well, you. This includes your emotions, goals, desires, worries, and needs so you can develop a sense of what you will take with you and what you may want to leave behind as you transition to being a new stepmom.

Think of the people (or person) who influenced you when you were growing up. Who are you picturing in your mind? Write about them in the space on this page. Think about what they taught you about raising children and embracing who you are as a person. Explore what you admired about those people and what you may want to emulate from how they raised you.

When you envisioned what being a stepmom would be like, what did you imagine? What are some of the expectations you had for yourself? What expectations did you have for your partner? What expectations did you have for the child(ren)? Write about these. Understanding your expectations will help you communicate your needs with the people in your life.

EXERCISE

Practicing Mindfulness

Find a quiet place where you won't be distracted. Close your eyes and focus on your breathing. Feel your chest rising and falling. Notice any pressure, pain, or tension in your body. You're increasing your awareness and connection to yourself at this moment. Now, take yourself to one of your favorite memories from your childhood. Focus on the details from the colors you see, the smells you're taking in, and maybe the sound of a person's voice from your memory. Enjoy this moment for a few minutes. Notice what feelings or thoughts this moment evokes for you.

Now, reflect on your favorite childhood memory from the "Practicing Mindfulness" exercise on page 4. Write down a description of that memory in as much detail as possible. Come back to this memory to help re-create that happiness and connect to your inner child whenever you need a little pick-me-up!

Write about some of the things you heard or wish you had heard from your caregivers while you were growing up. Based on your experiences, what advice would you give your younger self now? What would you tell or teach yourself about parenting? How can you use these experiences to help you in your new role as a stepmom?

EXERCISE

Letter of Reflection

As you've spent time thinking about the caregiving you received as a child, reflect on what you would like to say to those caregivers now. On a separate piece of paper, write a letter to them. What do you want to take from what they taught you? What do you never want to repeat? Tell them what type of stepparent you want to be. You don't have to send this to anyone unless you'd like to. This letter is just for you, to acknowledge your past and reflect on what is shaping you as a parent.

Our brains are wired to focus on what could go wrong, so let's focus instead on what you are most excited about when it comes to being a stepmom. What are the positives you see coming from this transition? How can you bring more excitement to any concerns you might have and use them as growth opportunities? For example, if you're worried the transition to living in the same home will be difficult, you might also look at this as an opportunity to let the kids help make it feel more like home.

EXERCISE

A Vision for Your Family

Let's make a vision board! Rather than forcing an image of what you think your family should be, use this exercise to see what comes to you about being a stepmom. The next time you're at the store, pick up two or three magazines that stand out to you. Cut out any words or pictures, without judgment, that seem meaningful to you. Tape or glue them on poster board and watch your vision for yourself and your family come together. Allow your creative expression to take center stage. Alternatively, you can put together a free Pinterest or web collage board or print inspiring images or words you find online. If you feel comfortable, you can have each family member make one, too, or make a family board together.

How did creating a vision board feel for you? Were you resistant to starting the project, or was it fun and exciting? Take some time to explore and write down the feelings you had while thinking about, preparing for, and putting together your vision board. Were you surprised by anything you found on your vision board? If so, why?

EXERCISE

Energized Movement

Movement helps us create physical and emotional energy. You've spent this first section getting reacquainted with your past and building dreams for the future. Now, let's take those dreams and thoughts and turn them into motion. Take yourself on a stroll through your neighborhood. Look at the houses or buildings, see the trees, and take big, deep breaths of air. You can make this inspiring walk a regular practice when you need to create action for your plans. Moving your body regularly can change your frame of mind. If you aren't able to walk around your neighborhood for any reason, enjoy the fresh air through an open window or mindfully meditate in a beautiful park.

Nothing can dim the light which shines from within.

—Maya Angelou

EXERCISE

Self-Exploration Meditation

Find a comfortable spot in your home—this could be a chair or your bed—anywhere you won't be disturbed. Sink into your chair and slow down your breath while breathing in through your nose and out through your mouth. Think about events and experiences in your life that once scared you, but which you survived. Visualize those experiences in your mind. What happened? What did you learn about yourself or take away from those experiences? What are you more capable of doing now that you weren't before?

Reflecting on your past experiences from the "Self-Exploration Meditation" (page 13), think about some strengths you've developed throughout your life that helped you get through those times. Write about those strengths and what they mean to you now. Is there a part of you that struggles to recognize your strengths? If so, why? What can you do to embrace your strengths more fully?

Think about the resources you have, such as friends, family, or a therapist. Who are the people in your life who support you? How often do you spend time with the people who make you feel capable and help you see your strengths? What are the potential barriers that might keep you from accessing those resources and people? Answer these questions on this page and write about how you can increase the presence of these resources in your life.

What do you do on a daily basis that reminds you of your strengths? What are some things in your environment that remind you to slow down, be inspired, or keep going? For example, do you meditate daily to work on controlling worrisome thoughts, or do you write in a journal about your emotions? Write down some ways you can add more of these methods to your daily routine—and then put them into practice!

What are you doing when you feel happiest? Who is around you? What are you wearing? Where are you? How can you replicate those moments more frequently in your life?

EXERCISE

What's Your Story?

We all develop stories in our minds to manage our expectations, fears, or even our happiness. Take a moment to think about the stories you've been telling yourself about being a stepmom. An example may be, *The kids will hate me, and I won't have enough time or energy to connect with them.* Let's explore where those stories come from. What might you need to see, feel, or experience to create a new, positive story where there is a negative one? Write them in the space provided.

....

....

....

....

....

....

What areas of your life do you think you need to grieve and let go of, in terms of painful memories, expectations, or fears? What might be holding you back from creating the family you dream of having? Explore what makes it difficult to let go of these things, and write about how you can use these experiences to move forward.

There's a familiar saying: "You can't pour from an empty cup." It's hard to give to others if you don't take time to replenish yourself. If your cup sometimes feels empty, what's keeping you from spending time doing the things you love? How do you feel about giving yourself permission to take the time for these things? On this page, write down two to three things that replenish you and at least one way you can make more time for them in your life.

EXERCISE

Write Your Own Biography

You've done a lot of soul-searching in this section. Write a brief description of your unique self, including the things you've learned about yourself, where you're going, and what your values and expectations are for the future. You can even attach a favorite photo—of just you, of you and your partner, or, of you and your new family!

....

....

....

....

....

....

....

....

....

....

EMBRACE WHO YOU ARE

As you've explored your background history, goals, strengths, and fears, you've learned a lot about yourself. Is there anything that feels like it is missing in your life right now? What has kept you from having that as a part of your life? Is there a practice you can implement in your life, like daily journaling or meditation, that helps you feel connected to yourself?

While thinking about who you are and who you want to become, think what would it look like to keep your identity and embrace who you are and what you love while becoming a new stepmom. Some women connect with support groups or friends, take time alone once a month to do something just for them, or journal daily to check in on themselves and their needs. What might work for you?

After working through this section, what clarity have you gained about yourself? What do you think about how you think and behave that you're taking away from this section? What are the small shifts you want to make in your daily life that incorporate what you've learned so far?

My daily emotional and physical needs are just as important as everyone else's.

Just start. Don't worry that you don't have all the answers yet.

—Alli Webb

SECTION 2

DEFINE YOUR NEW ROLE

You've spent a lot of time and energy thinking about who you are. Now it's time to shift gears toward defining your new role as a woman, partner, and stepparent. Many of us set expectations for ourselves that we've never fully clarified, yet the stakes feel really high! It's important to clearly define for yourself, your partner, and the children what your thoughts, hopes, and expectations are for this season of your lives. This section will offer prompts and exercises that will bring clarity to your new role in this family. Will you be a mentor, friend, or disciplinarian? What does being a stepmom mean for you? How will your role change over time? Well, you're about to find out!

EXERCISE

Who's Responsible?

To know what needs to adapt and shift in our life and relationships, we first have to evaluate what it is we are doing, what our partner is doing, and what we expect of our children. Using the table on page 29, walk yourself through a typical day from the time you wake up until you go to sleep. In the first column, list the responsibilities you take care of in the family. Use the second column to list what your partner's responsibilities are. In the third column, write what the children's responsibilities are. Think about what may need to shift, be added, or changed to this list to make it balanced. Use this list to inform yourself and your family about the roles and responsibilities that may need to shift and change.

YOUR RESPONSIBILITIES	YOUR PARTNER'S RESPONSIBILITIES	YOUR CHILD(REN)'S RESPONSIBILITIES
EX. FOLDING THE LAUNDRY	*EX. TAKING OUT THE TRASH/RECYCLING*	*EX. LOADING THE DISHWASHER*

You've taken some time to evaluate who does what in your family and how you feel about that structure (page 29). Of the responsibilities you are handling, what would you want to eliminate or add due to its impact on you or the family as a whole? How might you change those roles and responsibilities for yourself, your partner, and the children to feel a better balance or shift in responsibilities? Think about what would provide a better sense of balance to the family unit or reduce tension with scheduling conflicts. Why do those need to change, and what would that look like? Who would do what and when?

Our physical body often feels emotions before our brain makes the connection; we may operate on impulse before really being able to communicate what is going on for us. Have you ever felt easily on edge or overwhelmed? Write down three instances where you've found yourself reacting rather than thinking clearly, then write down one thing you can change about your routine so that you don't feel so easily overwhelmed.

Creating time just for you to relax can take minutes from your day but add energy that lasts much longer. Write down the last time you took a few minutes for yourself that made you feel more energized. What did you do? How can you incorporate more moments like that into your day-to-day life?

EXERCISE

Connect with Your Partner

Plan a time with your partner this week when the two of you can sit down uninterrupted. This could be anytime, like after the kids are asleep or during sports practice. Ask your partner what their hopes, dreams, and expectations are for your role in their children's lives and at home in this current season of your life together. Practice being a nonjudgmental listener by taking notes in the space provided.

What are your thoughts and feelings about your partner's hopes, dreams, and expectations (see "Connect with Your Partner," page 33)? Did it bring up anything for you that the two of you may need to talk more about? What do you feel their hopes, dreams, and expectations say about you? You can use these answers to deepen the communication of your feelings and needs with your partner in future conversations.

It may not have been easy to listen patiently to your partner's feelings, needs, and desires regarding your role and responsibilities. Of the things your partner listed for you on page 33, what would you want to eliminate, add, or change? Why? What can you both do to make positive changes based on your partner's comments?

EXERCISE

Motion Balances Emotion

Time to move your body! Our bodies can hold so much tension when we're stressed or overwhelmed, making it hard for us to process difficult emotions. Pick your favorite place in your home, backyard, or neighborhood. Put a time on your calendar this week where you can take some time alone to move your body in any way that feels good to you, and process your feelings by naming emotions that are present for you in this season of your life. Moving our bodies allows us to change our headspace and makes room for more positive energy and clarity.

Imagine that you and your partner are sitting down together. Think about the headspace you want to be in and how you hope the time together will go. On this page, write a letter to your partner that articulates your hopes, dreams, and expectations of your new role as a stepparent and what you would want those responsibilities to look like. Be open to sharing it with your partner. If you like, write down their responses, as well as any steps you both can take to achieve those goals.

DEFINE YOUR NEW ROLE

How our partner responds to us is extremely important. We can get really caught up in our emotional response to certain things that were said or unsaid. How did you feel about your partner's response? How did you feel supported? Was there anything you needed that you may not have gotten? Are there things you need to go back and talk about, or do you need outside support to address these issues?

EXERCISE

Blended Family Affirmations

Think of five to seven affirmations that represent how you would like your family to live as a unit. These affirmations can validate the role you have in one another's lives, the way you share information, and how you interact in a way that reflects your family's values. For example, "Our family spends time regularly together that is fun and purposeful."

Did you find yourself struggling to come up with positive affirmations about the family? Take some time to explore what emotions came up for you when thinking about growing into the role of stepmom and what that looks like for you. Reflect in the space on this page.

EXERCISE

Display Your Goals

Get your creative juices flowing! You can even include your partner and the kids, if you'd like. Write down or type the affirmations you explored in the last exercise (page 39), and put them in a beautiful frame, if you have one. Place the affirmations in an area of the house where everyone can see. Every time you walk past those affirmations, it will remind you of your commitment to one another.

Sometimes it can feel like, despite our best efforts as a stepparent, nothing is going according to plan. Having a friend outside the family to share our feelings with can help bring perspective and reduce loneliness and discouragement. What supportive qualities do you need in a friend right now? Who are the people in your life you can count on? When was the last time you reached out to them?

EXERCISE

Finding Extra Support

The best of intentions for ourselves, times with our partner, or communication with our children can go awry. Select an online or Facebook support group, a therapist you trust, or a local religious, spiritual, or community group in your area that offers parenting support. Set up a time to meet and share the affirmations you wrote for your family. Address the concerns you may have about your new role, and what type of accountability and support you need from that person. Accountability means setting goals knowing someone will check in on your progress and provide encouragement along the way. Check out the Resources section on page 167 for support group and therapy resources.

Checking in with your role as a stepmom and your feelings about it can often help with reducing frustration and communicating needs. How often do you hope to evaluate your role? What might you look for, to know it is time to reflect with yourself, your partner, or the kids? Looking ahead, how might you structure check-ins and with whom? Write your answers in the space provided.

A partner and kids sometimes means an ex-partner is involved. Do you have any concerns involving your interaction with the ex-partner? Does your partner know about your concerns? If not, what keeps you from sharing them? If so, is there any additional support you may need from your partner?

If you have children of your own, what concerns do you have when it comes to your role as their parent? Are your expectations different for yourself with them as opposed to your stepchildren? If so, how? Do you think anything needs to change in your approach?

Being pulled in different directions, feeling like you have to be one way with one person and a different way with another, can be challenging! What would it be like to feel congruous among all your relationships? Are there certain values you have that guide you in your interactions? For example, if you value compassion, do you provide the same level of grace or compassion toward yourself and family members?

> *Though everything has changed, I am still more me than I've ever been.*
>
> —Iain Thomas

What kind of self-care do you currently have in place to make sure you're getting the support, care, and time you need during this transition? How regularly are you accessing those resources? Is there anything missing in that plan that you might want to include?

There can be a lot of pressure on moms to appear strong. Most moms (step or not) often don't want to burden their family members with their feelings. But your feelings are important, too! How often are you and your partner checking in with one another? How often would you like to check in? What's one way you can draw closer to your partner for support in the weeks ahead?

EXERCISE

Relationship Education

The road ahead will be filled with great moments and imperfections. We can have the best intentions for success and all the hope in the world, but we still need to put in the work. I tell my clients to invest a minimum of 12 hours per year into education about themselves and their relationship with their partner. Families can do that through monthly check-ins with a counselor, reading a book together, or attending a class on relationships. Grab your calendars and book one hour a month that is just for the two of you and create some ideas for education that fit your needs as a family as well as your budget. For more information on couples therapy or free support groups, please check the Resources section on page 166.

Understanding when I need help and asking for it is a sign of strength.

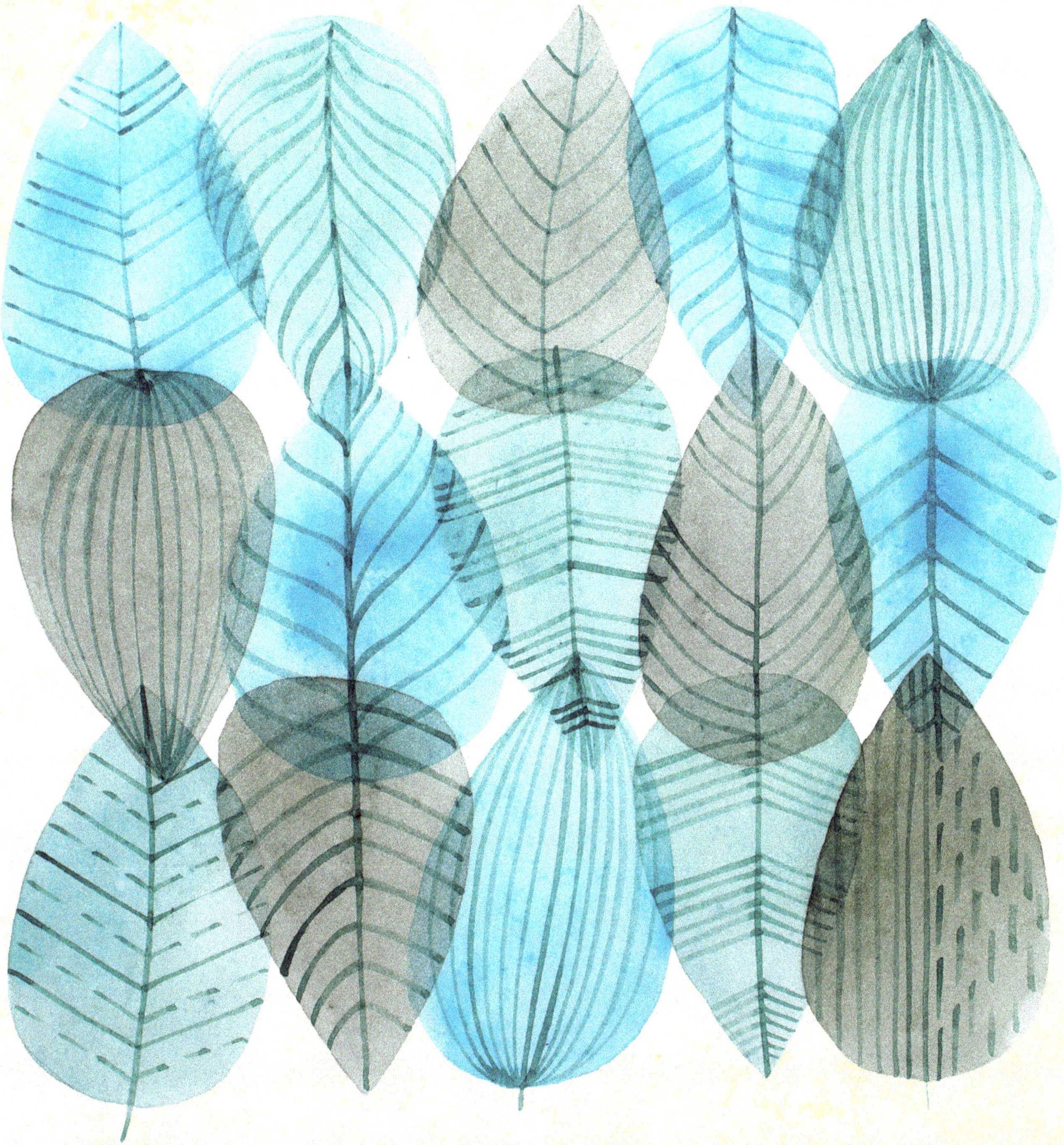

Self-acceptance is my refusal to be in an adversarial relationship to myself.

—Nathaniel Branden

SECTION 3

FOSTERING PATIENCE AND COMPASSION

You try so hard to be everything for everyone; to have it all together, to know what is going to happen down the road, with a solution waiting. Unfortunately, life is messy, and trying to control every situation is futile because unexpected things happen all the time. We all have those moments where everything feels like it is falling apart, and you can't seem to do what needs to be done or feel what you would hope to feel. Emotions can get tangled and in the way, especially when it comes to navigating relationships with co-parents and children. This section will walk you through various exercises to help you better connect with yourself, release control, and have empathy for yourself and your family members. The prompts will get to the heart of fostering self-compassion and respect.

Take a moment to write your own definition of "compassion." How well do you demonstrate compassion toward yourself, your partner, and your kids? Do you find it easier to be compassionate toward one person over another? What do you think makes compassion difficult? Write down one way you might grow in this area or toward that specific person. For example, "I can acknowledge what is being done well first before moving on to what needs to change."

EXERCISE

Just Breathe

When things feel overwhelming, that's when you know you need more self-compassion. Feeling overwhelmed is how your body lets you know it can't release tension and doesn't know what to do with all these feelings at once. This simple breathing exercise, which I call 3-4-5-6 breath, can help. (If this is difficult for you, try breathing in through your mouth and out through your nose in a slow and calming rhythm.)

1. Start by taking a deep breath in through your nose for a count of four.

2. Hold that breath for a count of five.

3. Release that breath through your mouth for a count of six.

4. Repeat this three times.

No matter where you are or what is going on, this breathing exercise can redirect your focus, help you gain a sense of control, and bring stability back into the situation.

We can have the best of intentions and the most elaborately laid-out plans only to watch unforeseen things pop up. What is your ideal preference for handling changes to your expectations or plans? On this page, reflect on how you developed your ideal skills or tools for managing change and who modeled them to you.

You may have had to navigate changes to your expectations and plans many times throughout your life. Take a moment to think about those times when expectations and plans changed. How did you navigate them? Did you use your ideal tools for managing change (page 58)? What did you learn from some of those instances that you can take with you into new changes that arise?

EXERCISE

Get Grounded

Grab your favorite comforting drink, like tea, coffee, or water. Now, go to a quiet place in your home or neighborhood, leaving behind or shutting off your phone. As you're holding the drink, think about what you feel in your hands. Is it cold? Is it hot? Take in your surroundings. What sounds do you hear? What do you smell? As you drink your beverage, what do you taste? Using your senses helps ground you to the here and now, refocusing your attention on yourself and your experience. You can use this grounding tool anywhere you go to recenter yourself and clear out any overwhelming feelings or experiences.

When you're feeling low or stuck, a great question to ask yourself is, "What would I tell a friend in this same situation?" Reflect on a stressful situation or a change to your expectations that happened recently. What would you tell a friend going through that experience? Write that answer on this page, but address it to yourself.

I think that one of these days . . . you're going to have to find out where you want to go. And then you've got to start going there.

—J. D. Salinger

EXERCISE

Taking Time for You

Take a moment to think about where you were and who you were with the last time you had some fun and felt truly refreshed. You can reflect on that moment to re-create those feelings, or you can try something new with a friend or family member that you've always wanted to try. Grab your phone, text your friend, pick a place, and set up your reservations. Self-compassion means allowing yourself a break from always having to be "on." Spending time with friends and having fun is a great way to show yourself that you matter, too.

As discussed earlier, it's important to continually check in with your partner. What compassionate words of support do you need from your partner right now? When do you need to hear those words from your partner (i.e., right now, in certain situations, etc.)? Keeping compassionate acts and words in mind, how might you let your partner know about your needs? How can you ask about theirs?

Many times, moms may not give themselves permission to think about what they want. The focus is often on the needs of their family. Explore what it is like for you to give yourself permission to enjoy an added luxury, like a long bath on Sundays or a movie night with your friends. Write down three things you enjoy doing but haven't done in a while.

EXERCISE

Envisioning Happiness

Did you know that your body can't determine if something has happened, is happening, or will happen? It just knows what information you're feeding it right now. For example, if you are visualizing a heartwarming memory—for example, maybe you're thinking about the beach in detail—your brain will respond with emotions that match that experience. Take a moment to envision your happiest place or memory. Use your senses or imagination to describe the scene to yourself in the chart on page 67. This activity allows you to find peace, happiness, patience, and compassion at any moment you need it.

SENSE	SCENE
Taste	
Smell	
Touch	
Sound	
Sight	

Joy and happiness can be scary emotions, because we're sometimes afraid they won't last. Allowing yourself to feel and express happiness with yourself and others brings joyful connection. When the fear arises that happiness may not last, showing yourself compassion helps connect you to your humanness. Write down one joyful moment you are afraid of, and reflect on how you can show yourself compassion in that situation, like repeating an affirmation of love toward yourself.

Do you struggle to permit yourself to do things you enjoy after a difficult day or situation? If not, why not? If so, how so? How might you incorporate even more joy into a difficult or busy day to lighten the burden of stress? For example, you may really enjoy snuggling in bed watching your favorite show, or having your partner clean up the dinner dishes.

EXERCISE

Active Visualization

This active visualization exercise gives you the ability to control what emanates from you in a moment of hardship. Close your eyes and pick a color, or even a pleasurable feeling. Imagine that color or feeling filling up your body, starting with your feet and moving up to your forehead. That color or feeling can represent compassion and love. When feeling anxious, angry, or frustrated, allow yourself to see your body filling with that color or pleasurable feeling as you breathe in and out. Allow yourself to exude that color as a form of love and compassion.

We often get angry or upset when we have no control over a situation; perhaps you've experienced this while blending your family. How do you define control? How do you generally find control in changing situations and expectations? How do you feel about your definition and use of control? What can improve that definition or use? For example, you might feel relaxed, at peace, and in control when everything is in order and the house is clean.

EXERCISE

Positive Reframing

No matter what you do or how positive you try to be, negative thoughts toward yourself or others are going to arise. As you learn to suspend judgment, notice when those thoughts are present. When you notice a negative thought, stop it, and in its place say something compassionate to yourself or about the situation. An example might be, "I acknowledge I'm feeling sad, but I have options and I trust in the connections I have around me." This doesn't mean you always have to feel positive; it means you have an opportunity to pay attention to what your mind is telling you and choose what to believe instead. Come up with one or two replacement phrases to use when your negative thoughts arise.

Change takes time, and patience is crucial for managing your perspective on how your blended family operates. How do you define patience? How do you experience patience with yourself or others in difficult situations? How can your definition of patience expand to create more space for natural reactions and the messiness of dealing with change? For example, patience might mean allowing yourself to cry when you feel overwhelmed, or asking for help from your partner.

A healthy and mutual respect for all persons in the home can soothe tensions and allow for more expressive communication. Respect can also help build patience and compassion. What is your definition of respect? On this page, write down at least two ways you experience that from your partner and children. Next, write down at least two ways they experience respect from you.

Expressing feelings and needs can be difficult for many people, especially when merging one family with another and factoring in each new personality. Others may express themselves in ways that are different from your expression of feelings or needs. For example, you might believe some thoughts should be kept to oneself, whereas someone else might need to have their feelings heard. Write down some ways your family members express themselves differently, and list examples of how you can allow them to do that even if you disagree.

People, ourselves included, are going to mess up. Blending families and change takes time and effort to work out routines, schedules, and everyone's needs and feelings. How do you define grace? How do you extend grace to yourself, your partner, and your children?

Now that you have defined grace, patience, and control for yourself and explored how they relate to your blending family, think about whether there is a need to change, broaden, or redefine your ideas of patience, compassion, and respect. If yes, why? What are some changes you can make? For example, you might choose to use affirmations to grow in grace when you're feeling really hard on yourself.

EXERCISE

Personal Affirmations

In the last exercise (page 72), you focused on noticing your thoughts and choosing what you believe. Now let's add 10 unique, compassionate affirmations for yourself. For example, "I am patient with those around me and can take space to calm down if I need it." Repeat these to yourself regularly so they become your go-to thoughts in difficult moments.

In what specific ways can you see yourself practicing increased compassion, patience, respect, and grace for yourself, your partner, and children in your day-to-day interactions? Think about how you might encourage your partner and children to practice those values in their interactions with one another as well.

I am allowing myself
to be imperfect and
recognize I am doing
the best I can every day.

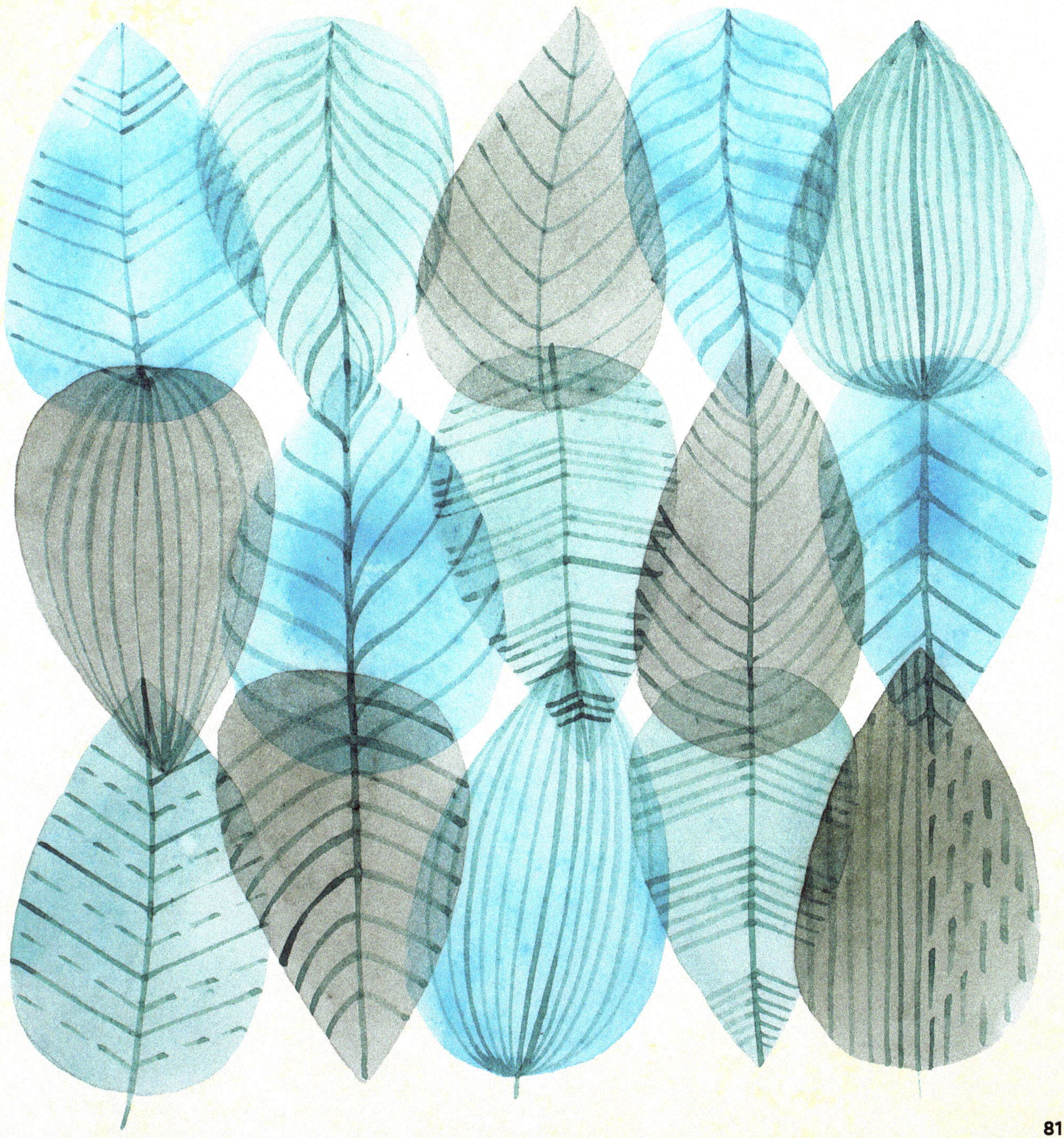

Setting boundaries is an act of love towards yourself and an act of respect towards others.

—Lisa Olivera

SECTION 4

EVERYONE BENEFITS FROM BOUNDARIES

As a stepmom in a blending family, setting boundaries is one of the most important steps you can take. It's true that everyone benefits from boundaries. To have the emotional and physical energy to accomplish all your goals requires setting boundaries. Throughout this section, we will explore what boundaries are, assess your parenting style (because everyone is unique), learn how to co-parent and what discipline is, manage conflict, deal with struggles and failures, and, finally, build trust and connection with your partner and children. Many people believe that setting boundaries pertains only to what we don't want. The prompts and exercises in this section will teach you just how good boundaries can be—for you, your partner, and the children—to not only build but also maintain closeness.

Before we can build on something, we must first know our foundation. How would you define the term "boundaries"? Where did you develop that definition? When you think about building boundaries, what emotions come up for you and why?

Think of some boundaries you've had to place with your stepchildren. How did you set those boundaries? What was the response? Is there anything happening currently that gives you pause when considering setting new boundaries?

EVERYONE BENEFITS FROM BOUNDARIES

EXERCISE

What Are You Okay With?

Boundaries can be defined as what is okay versus what is not okay in a given situation, expectations, or conversation. On page 87 you will see two columns. Pick one issue that has been bothering you regarding your children. In the first column, write down what is okay about this issue. In the next column, write down what is not okay about this issue. For example, the issue may be how you are spoken to by your stepchildren. In the first column, you might write, "It's okay to have and express feelings." In the second column, you might say, "It's not okay to use hateful words and slam the door." This exercise will help you communicate your boundaries with others in future interactions.

ISSUE	WHAT IS OKAY?	WHAT IS NOT OKAY?

EVERYONE BENEFITS FROM BOUNDARIES

Boundary setting can sometimes manifest in challenging ways. When we focus solely on behavior, however, we're generally looking at a symptom and not the cause. What bothersome behavior have you noticed with your stepchildren lately? Maybe your stepchild is locking themselves in their room, or seeming easily frustrated and unwilling to engage. Consider what other emotions they might be feeling, like fear or loneliness. Have you ever experienced that same behavior? What was the story behind it?

EXERCISE

Exploring Parenting Styles

Everyone has different parenting styles. Some people may be more stern, placing high expectations on their children, some may be softer and more forgiving, and others may ignore their children's behavior altogether. In this exercise, visit some public spaces, sit outside on your porch, or sit near the local bus stop and observe how other families are interacting. Take in what you notice about the various behaviors in children, and notice how the parents respond. What behaviors did you feel were unacceptable? What responses did you feel were helpful or unhelpful? Did you notice anything positive resulting from clear boundaries?

Negative emotions, like overwhelm, sadness, or fear, can affect the stories we tell ourselves and the ways in which we interact with others. For example, when I'm overwhelmed, I might think, *No one really wants to help me. I have to do everything around here by myself.* Instead, tell yourself a story that supports your needs, like, *I know I can ask for help if I really need it instead of doing this alone.* Write a few supportive stories you can repeat to yourself when needed.

Co-parenting is as difficult a challenge as stepparenting. With everyone needing, expecting, and wanting different things, it can be easy for tempers to flare and judgments and/or assumptions to be made. Are you giving energy to something in a co-parenting relationship that isn't getting much positive return, like progress or change in a given situation? What are the things you're feeling, saying, or doing that are draining you when you're with the co-parent? If repeating yourself isn't working, explore alternative ways to communicate a boundary that may not include talking. This can look like changing expectations or not engaging in conversation that doesn't go anywhere.

EXERCISE

Sharing Co-Parenting Boundaries

Setting boundaries is rarely an easy or quick process. Identifying and sharing boundaries that honor your energy and resources while leaving room for flexibility is an art, not a science. Let's practice how to share a boundary. In the chart on page 93, write down the behavior that is challenging with your co-parent. Then, write down what may be okay or understandable about it. Finally, write down the positively stated need you have that would showcase change. For example, let's say the behavior is not having a structured bedtime for the child. Your positively stated need might be, "I know spending time with Billy is important for you. Mike and I would like to coordinate with you on a consistent bedtime for Billy to follow at both homes." You can use these practice boundaries to prepare you for future conversations with the co-parent. Including your partner in this exercise builds a sense of teamwork, *further supporting your co-parenting.*

CHALLENGING BEHAVIOR	WHAT'S OKAY	YOUR NEEDS

Regardless of whether setting boundaries with a co-parent is smooth or difficult, the practice of checking in with yourself and setting boundaries with others is a necessity for protecting your energy. What is your routine for checking in with yourself? What improvements can be made in that routine so you can count on it?

EXERCISE

Emotional Coaching

We can use emotional coaching to identify an issue with a child and bring education, guidance, and the establishment of healthy boundaries. Try the steps on this page after a missed expectation or a blowup at the dinner table. Make sure you and your child are calm and there has been some time to reflect beforehand.

1. Help your child identify their emotions.
2. Use empathy to connect to their emotions.
3. Ask about some other ways they can handle those emotions next time.
4. Make a plan together.

(continued on next page)

For example, let's say your child is having meltdowns about doing chores:

1. *I wonder if you're feeling angry about doing your chores because you're tired after school?*

2. *I get it! When I'm tired, chores are the last thing I feel like doing.*

3. *What are some other things you can do or say when you're angry or tired?*

4. *Next time you're tired or upset, tell Mom/Dad or me that you need a few minutes in your room to calm down and give us a time when you will have your chores done that day.*

As you think about disciplining your stepchildren, what thoughts, feelings, or concerns come up for you? Take time to explore what you believe healthy discipline is and from whom you learned the most effective strategies. Reflect on those insights on this page. Knowing how you want to feel after an interaction involving discipline will set the tone for how you approach it.

Daring to set boundaries is about having the courage to love ourselves even when we risk disappointing others.

—Brené Brown

Navigating boundaries with your children, partner, and any co-parents involved is bound to bring up conflict. How would you define conflict, and what are your general thoughts on navigating conflict? What is the role you take when conflict is present? How did you learn that role, and are you comfortable with it?

EXERCISE

Conflict Resolution

When in conflict with your partner or children, keep in mind that there are two sides to every story, and both are valid. The next time a conflict arises, put yourself in the role of listener first. A good listener keeps eye contact, asks open-ended questions, summarizes what they've heard, and offers validation—seeking to understand the other person, even if they don't agree. Below are some sample questions and validating statements. Come up with some of your own to ask your partner or stepchild in your next heated interaction.

Is there a story behind this for you?

Why is this so important to you?

What is your preferred outcome here?

It must be challenging to consider these options . . .

I get that it's . . .

Take a moment to reflect on your role as listener. Think about your last heated interaction with your partner or child. What did you learn about this person as you listened to their side? What were your internal feelings or responses? For example, did you find it difficult to have empathy because you disagreed with what they said? What was it like to suspend your judgment for a short time?

EVERYONE BENEFITS FROM BOUNDARIES

EXERCISE

Move Your Body!

Learning and trying new things can increase tension and a host of other emotions because our body doesn't know how to react to the situation yet. To clear your mind and help you set boundaries more empathetically, try moving your body in a way that feels good for you and allows you to release the stored-up tension. For example, if you hold tension in your shoulders, shrug them when you're tense. If you're ashamed, try elongating your spine. Any small movement, like moving your eyes, moving your head from side to side, or tapping your finger works, too!

As you've been exploring setting boundaries, are there any fears or hesitations coming up for you? Write them down on this page. Explore any contradicting feelings around boundary setting. For example, "I'm excited to practice this, but I am afraid of how my partner will react."

EVERYONE BENEFITS FROM BOUNDARIES

Boundaries can be very challenging to get right. As you're learning, so are your partner and stepchildren. Practicing grace toward yourself in this learning process can look like managing your mindset through positive affirmations. Think about some nice things you can say to yourself when setting boundaries, like, "It's okay that I'm still learning. I will always keep trying." Write at least three positive affirmations on this page.

EXERCISE

Mindful Breathing

Setting boundaries means taking time for yourself to release tension and anxiety. Sit in a quiet space on the floor next to a wall or another hard surface. Place your right hand on your heart and your left hand on your belly. Take a big, deep breath in and feel your heart and belly expand. Release your breath through your mouth and feel your heart and belly contract back in. Do this several times until you feel tension release. Notice any compassion toward yourself coming back, and remain focused on learning from the situation you envisioned and how you may handle a similar situation differently next time.

Healthy boundaries involve trust. Building trust with yourself and others comes through intentional and consistent effort. What areas of your life and relationships need more intention and consistency? Maybe you need a date night every week with your partner or a journal in which to express your thoughts before speaking them out loud. What can you do to improve the consistency in your interactions with others to promote trust?

What are you doing and who are you with when you feel the most connected to yourself? How might you be more intentional and consistent in your interactions with your children, partner, and co-parent to help further your connection with them?

Think about what you might need right now, or who might offer connection and support to help you build healthier boundaries and connectedness. Who do you know in your life that has good boundaries? Can you talk to them? Make a plan to reach out to that person for support and have them hold you accountable in setting and keeping your boundaries.

Now that you have explored boundary setting, how have your views on boundaries changed? How have they stayed the same? What is one step you can take in the next week to build healthier boundaries?

Boundaries are an act of love toward myself and a way to teach others how to love me.

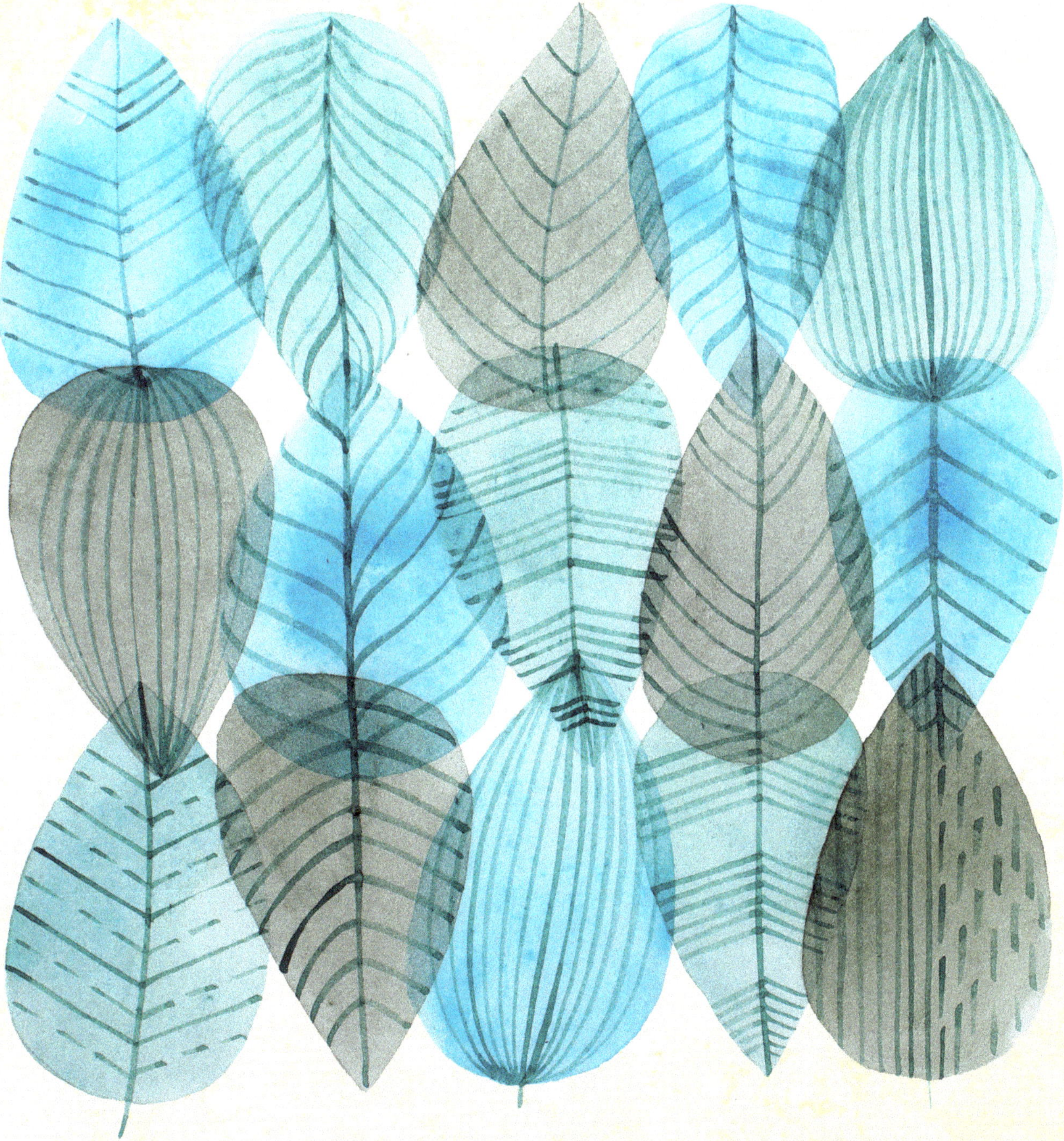

What comes easy won't last long, and what lasts long won't come easy.

—Francis Kong

SECTION 5

NURTURE YOUR RELATIONSHIPS

You've embarked on this chapter in your life as stepmom because of your love for and commitment to your partner. It can become very easy to let your children's needs take precedence in the relationship, but to build safety and security in the relationship for everyone involved, the relationship with your partner must take center stage. In this section, the prompts and exercises will help you explore what makes up a healthy relationship with your partner, how to build fun and engagement in your lives as a couple, and how to strengthen as a couple to be the best parents you can be. Let's dive in!

In preparation for blending your lives and families, what did you imagine your life together would look like? How did you imagine spending time together? Did you expect to be able to prioritize your relationship with the demands of parenthood? Do you feel like you are living up to those expectations? If so, in what ways? If not, what is keeping you from doing so?

C: I imagined that we would have normal family struggles, but overall be happy and work as a team. I imagined we'd spend time w/ the kids or after they were asleep or w/ dads. I thought we would be able to prioritize our relationship. I don't feel like we're doing a great job at doing that. We let the kids stay up late so we have very little time at the end of the night.

B: I imagined our lives to be more cohesive between the kids than how it actually is. I expected us to have more quality time as a couple. I expected to be able to prioritize our relationship pretty easily (seeing as we were doing that pretty easily long distance). I could do a better job at being more intentional when we get quality time as a couple.

THE BLENDED FAMILY JOURNAL FOR STEPMOMS

EXERCISE

Getting Intentional

Many couples assume the amount of time they spend with one another is important. In my experience, it's the intentional quality time you spend together that counts. Plan a time with your partner away from the children to explore items from the list on this page. Choose the ones that are meaningful to incorporate into your everyday life. Discuss how you plan to follow through on these actions.

Ideas for Connection:

- Leaving one another sticky notes or sending text messages to say hello

- Checking in with one another throughout the day

- Engaging in intimacy through physical touch

- Managing stress or failures through empathy and kind words

- Dates and getaways (sometimes the best dates are at home when the kids are asleep)

After the last exercise (page 115), did you find yourself surprised by your partner's needs or wants when it comes to building connection points in the relationship? Were you surprised by what was important for you and how to incorporate it into your lives?

B: No and no - "let's skip this page"

C: No, I'm not surprised by needs or wants from Brianna or by what was important for me.

Expressing your appreciation for the people in your life is key to feeling seen, heard, and valued. This can build your relationship not only with your partner but also with your children. What are some things your partner and children have done that you've appreciated lately? What have your partner and stepchildren done that went unnoticed or unappreciated?

NURTURE YOUR RELATIONSHIPS

EXERCISE

Sharing Appreciation

Now that you've reflected on some things you appreciate in your relationships (page 117), let those people know! Our brains tend to focus on what we're not getting rather than the good things happening around us, so let's practice sharing appreciation. The goal is to do this exercise at least three times a day with your partner and your children.

1. Pick an adjective that describes the other person (e.g., kind, resourceful, helpful, thoughtful, trustworthy, etc.).

2. Put your adjective and a specific situation together into a clear appreciation. For example, *Thanks for doing the dishes today. That was helpful!*

3. Send this in a text, leave it in a voicemail or on a sticky note, or tell that person as soon as you see it happening.

Getting into the habit of appreciation can help you be more grateful for, and compassionate toward, your family. Have you found it challenging lately to focus on the good things? How well does your family offer and accept compliments? How can you help those who are hesitant to work on accepting and offering compliments?

NURTURE YOUR RELATIONSHIPS

EXERCISE

Express Your Needs

For many couples, expressing a need can come across as a criticism, if the need is focused on what we're *not* receiving from our partners. Let's look at how you can identify and positively express your needs.

1. Identify what you may be feeling at this moment. Write that emotion here: _____

2. If that emotion was negative, such as fearful or sad, think of its opposite, such as secure or happy.

3. What would allow you to feel or keep that positive emotion? For example, *I would feel more connected if my partner would put their phone down.*

4. Share the feeling you have or would like to have and be specific with what you want, rather than what you don't want. For example, *I'd feel connected to you right now if I could have your eye contact and engagement in planning our trip* or *I feel really happy just being in your arms like this without distraction.*

Explore your relationship with your own needs right now. What is it like for you to share your needs with others? Do you find yourself withholding or disconnecting from your needs, or are you comfortable when sharing your needs? How do others, like your partner or children, typically respond to your needs?

The expression of needs is generally learned from our caregivers. What do you remember about your caregivers expressing their needs with one another? Were there fights about what one person wanted or needed? Were they really in touch with one another, and openly expressing their needs? Do you carry any of those same patterns when it comes to expressing your needs? If so, what would you like to change about how you share your needs with others?

EXERCISE

Check In with Your Partner

Checking in with your partner daily in a nonjudgmental way is extremely important for maintaining healthy communication and staying connected to each other's day-to-day life. Every day, set aside 20 minutes just for you and your partner to connect about current stressors or issues outside of the relationship, such as work or hobbies.

Take turns being a listener and a speaker for 10 minutes each. When you're listening, practice setting aside your opinion and focusing on problem-solving. Ask questions about your partner's experience and provide empathy. Then switch roles. For added support, download the Gottman Card Deck app on your mobile device and use the different card deck options for asking better questions, expressing needs, and providing empathy (see the Resources on page 167 for more information).

Once you've started doing daily check-ins with your partner, reflect on whether you're becoming more connected. You can do this by writing down what you're learning about your partner. Do you know what is currently stressing your partner out? Do you feel like your partner knows what you're excited or worried about right now? Explore some of the issues in your life you'd like to share more of with your partner.

When you connect with others, how do you typically engage with them about what is going on in their lives? Are you often "busy," or open to them sharing more specific emotions and experiences? How do you feel about listening without problem-solving? What about that do you find challenging? How might you improve as a listener in your next conversation with your partner or stepchildren?

NURTURE YOUR RELATIONSHIPS

> The simple truth is that happy marriages are based on a deep friendship. By this, I mean mutual respect for and enjoyment of each other's company.
>
> —John Gottman

EXERCISE

Dream Letter

On a separate piece of paper, write a letter to yourself about the dreams you have for yourself. Use this as an opportunity to dream big about what you want and what is possible for you. Use present language to focus on the idea that it has happened. For example, "I feel good about my physical health and connected to my partner in meaningful ways." This helps your brain connect with the information and see it as possible because your brain will believe the information you feed it. Watch out for limiting beliefs like *This isn't possible* or *I don't believe this can happen*. This is an exercise of mindfulness and seeing opportunities, not roadblocks.

Dreaming allows us to stay connected with ourselves and keep out of survival mode. How often do you allow yourself to dream about what you want? Who do you share those dreams with? Who would you like to share your dreams with for support?

What are the dreams your partner and children have shared with you? Do you view those dreams as realistic possibilities? What may keep you from supporting those dreams in others? What dreams have you helped your partner and children pursue?

EXERCISE

Date Night

Gather your calendars and your current budget and plan a date night! With my clients, I recommend couples think about the ways in which they can connect with one another, as well as how often and for how long to spend that time together. Everyone's budgets and calendars are different, so this a time to get creative. Pick a time where you two can spend some time alone, even if it's 10 minutes at home, and mark it on the calendar. Identify people who can help with childcare or plan around visitation schedules. Get these dates on the calendar for the whole year. Even if things have to change, having a clear vision and intention will help you hit most of those targets.

After planning some date nights ("Date Night," page 130), reflect on what that experience was like for you and your partner. Did you notice any resistance on either end to setting aside intentional time for the relationship? Do you have any concerns about keeping these dates a priority? What can you cross off your calendar that could leave more room for these much-needed times away to focus on your relationship?

What are the dreams you and your partner have for your future as a couple, as parents, and as community contributors? What would be the next step toward being more involved in the community with your partner?

What does trust mean to you? In your opinion, how does trust evolve? How do a couple and family maintain trust?

NURTURE YOUR RELATIONSHIPS

EXERCISE

Trust Exercise

Trust is built through consistency and time. Often, getting married and trusting that our partner will be there with us through everything life throws at us is a leap of faith. There are multiple facets to building and maintaining trust. For the sake of having some fun and trying something new, get your partner and take turns navigating a room or household chore with your eyes closed, while the other person talks you through it. The goal of this exercise is to learn your fears and examine how you two work and rely on one another. Think about how other day-to-day tasks being accomplished or not may impact your trust for one another.

After completing the exercise on page 134, reflect on what it was like for you. What feelings did you have going into it? Were you able to complete the exercise? If so, what did you learn about yourself and your partner? If you didn't complete the exercise, what stopped you?

As we end this section, write down what you have learned about what it means to nurture a relationship. How do you plan on staying intentional in all of your relationships? Finally, reflect on how you plan to evolve and adapt as the relationships change through regular check-ins with yourself and those closest to you.

_____

_____

_____

_____

_____

_____

_____

_____

_____

_____

_____

_____

I am growing in respect and deeper understanding of my partner without judgment.

Take the first step in faith. You don't have to see the whole staircase, just take the first step.

—Martin Luther King Jr.

SECTION 6

NAVIGATE THE ROAD AHEAD

You've learned a lot since starting this journal, and I bet you have learned even more as you've become a stepmom. As we finish our time together, reflect on the lessons you've learned and the strategies you've practiced, and explore the path ahead, including the roadblocks you may encounter. Throughout this section, we will be pulling from all the themes we explored together to create steps forward. You will learn how to check in with yourself and how to make necessary changes as both you and your family evolve and grow. It's important to create new rituals and experiences as a family, but it's also important to explore your own interests, creativity, and community, and make time to check in with yourself each day. Track your own growth and discover new things about yourself. Enriching your life will help enrich your family's life. Have gratitude for the journey you and your family are taking. Above all else, stay true to who you are, and you'll be able to create a safe space for your family to grow, change, challenge each other, build strong connections, and learn from one another.

As you reflect on the time you've spent working through this journal and becoming a stepmom, what have you learned about yourself? How have these lessons shaped your expectations, needs, and responses to conflict with your children, partner, and yourself?

EXERCISE

Body Scan

Generally, our bodies speak to us about our emotions before our mind does. There is a simple tool called body scanning that can help you connect the mind and the body in order to slow down, listen to yourself, and check in on your needs. Practice this exercise when you notice tension or overwhelm. You can also use this daily to check in with yourself.

1. Sit in a comfortable spot and take a few deep breaths in and out.

2. Starting from your head and going down through your feet, notice any tension, pain, or pressure.

3. As you notice it, move that part of your body with your mind, and focus your breathing into that part.

Connecting an emotion to a sensation in your body can help reduce overwhelm because we have learned how our body manifests certain emotions and why. During the "Body Scan" exercise on page 141, where did you notice the tension or pressure in your body? What emotion(s) might be tied to it? How might noticing the sensations in your body help you connect more deeply to your emotional self on a daily basis?

You've put together a brand-new role for yourself as a stepmom with healthy expectations and boundaries. What has it been like for you to show up in that new role? Are you finding parts of it meaningful? Are you noticing any resistance from your family members?

How have your boundaries shifted lately? What have you been pulling your energy and time away from that is really important to you? What has been enhancing your energy? Are there still parts of your experience as a stepmom that are challenging? Take a moment to explore, with curiosity and compassion toward yourself, how these challenges may bring joy down the road.

EXERCISE

Check Your To-Dos

Checking off an item on a to-do list rewards your brain with a little shot of dopamine—the happy hormone! On this page you will see a list of some of the tools and exercises from this journal. Take a moment to write down some of the exercises from this journal you'd like to try in the coming month. Maybe you want to plan that date night, build your vision board, or take a walk in the park. If completing the entire activity feels too big, ask yourself what feels like a good first step toward that goal and write it down instead.

- Journaling
- Mindful meditation
- Body scan (page 141)
- Check-in with your partner (and yourself)
- ....
- ....
- ....
- ....

You can't do everything all at once. It's important to take what you have learned and prioritize the tools you use based on what you and your family need. Of the strategies you wrote down in the last exercise (page 145), what feels doable for you over the next week? Choose one and write down the steps you can take to accomplish it.

Breaking bigger tasks down into smaller steps helps avoid feelings of overwhelm. Even small steps are progress. What is the biggest change you see taking the most time to implement? What is one small thing you can do in the next month as a sign of progress toward that big goal?

EXERCISE

Know Your Values

Knowing what drives, motivates, and inspires you is key to staying true to yourself. Values are an individual's standards or principles for what is important in life. They are the lens through which we make decisions and judgments about our behaviors and those of other people. On this page, list your top three values and connect with them. For example, you might value love, peace, or connectedness. Picture a time when you felt you really embodied each of those values. Play out the scene in your mind and notice with curiosity what you feel and where you feel it in your body. Remember, your brain will respond as if this is happening right now, so this is a useful tool when you feel stuck or unmotivated.

1. _____

2. _____

3. _____

Naming your values can give you a sense of direction and focus. Usually when we feel off or overwhelmed, we're not living in alignment with our values. How might you incorporate your values (page 148) in your daily decision-making with your family and for yourself?

Living in alignment with our values requires us to prioritize where we put our time, energy, and focus. There is not enough time in the day, and we can't do it all! How are you prioritizing your focus and energy today? For example, if you value connection, how have you gone about making or seeking connection with others today? This can also be a good check-in question for daily journaling.

EXERCISE

An Activity Just for You

As mothers and partners, we often lose ourselves in fulfilling the needs of others, like our children, partner, and friends. We tend to put aside the things we used to do or have always wanted to do because they're not practical. In this exercise, pick one activity you have been putting off, one that is purely meant for pleasure, and go do it. Maybe it's getting your nails done, reading a book, watching a show you enjoy, joining a gym, or taking a bath. Whatever it is, make a plan in the space on this page for it to happen in the next week.

....

....

....

....

....

....

Thinking about yourself and giving yourself permission to do what makes you happy helps you feel more connected to yourself and others, more patient, and less resentful. Explore what giving yourself permission to love and nurture yourself would look like. For example, on this page, you might write, *I give myself permission to take a nature walk every week* or *I give myself permission to take a night off from making dinner.*

Taking an opportunity to dream about your future will help provide clarity in your decision-making and help you set intentions. Dreaming is all about giving yourself space to think about what the future holds and the idea that we have some control over what happens next. How do you feel about the concept of dreaming, and what do your dreams represent for you?

Challenges are gifts that force us to search for a new center of gravity. Don't fit them, just find a new way to stand.

—Oprah Winfrey

EXERCISE

Family Rituals

Rituals are events or times we can count on that help us connect, grow, and stay intentional in our relationships. On this page, list some things or activities that you and the family have been doing every day that you can count on. Next to each of those things, write a sentence of appreciation for that ritual and its meaning in your life. For example, "My partner kisses me goodbye every day. I appreciate how it makes me feel important to my partner." Appreciation for even the smallest things helps us not take ourselves or each other for granted.

Good things take time to build, and even noticing the small steps toward your new dream can help when things inevitably get hard. What are some ways you, your partner, and the children are making progress in spending time together? Thinking about the month ahead, what is one other ritual, like eating a meal without the TV on or planning a family movie night, that you and the family can do to promote closeness?

EXERCISE

Inspiration Journal

Daily journaling or making lists of your intentions, goal progress, and things you are grateful for helps you stay motivated and truly intentional in your life. Buy a notebook or journal that inspires you. Write your favorite quote from this book on the first page of the journal. Next, using the practices, techniques, and tips you've learned from this book, write progress check-in questions at the top of the first several pages of the journal. For example, "How well am I doing with showing grace to myself and others?" "What have I learned about my partner and stepchildren this week?" Or, "What can I do this next week that I've been putting off?"

Asking the right questions of ourselves can be difficult. We may feel discouraged and ashamed when we focus on what we didn't do instead of all that we tried. Many of us know what we need to do but find it difficult to start or continue the process. Are there any fears holding you back from what you want or need to do right now? Explore how shame plays a role in reducing your motivation.

Expanding your definition of success can be very useful in not letting shame get you down. Remember, even small progress is progress. Explore what success has meant to you in the past and how you might define success for yourself right now in a way that focuses on all that you are instead of all that you may not be yet. Use this new definition of success when you're being hard on yourself.

EXERCISE

Check In with Yourself

On your phone, set a calendar check-in for six months from today's date: _____

In that spot, write the following questions to ask yourself. Use these check-ins to be intentional with what needs to change in the following six months to support the values you wrote on page 148.

- What have I done well as a stepmom up to now?
- How have my relationships evolved with my stepchildren and partner?
- What support have I been getting?
- What support do I still need?
- What have I been doing for myself?
- What boundaries have I set that make me proud?
- What are my priorities and intentions in the next six months for myself, my relationship with my partner, and my relationship with my stepchildren?

Asking for help and surrounding yourself with trusted people and resources is crucial for accountability and support as you take on this new role of stepmom. Explore the supports that may be missing from your life right now, and what you are willing to try to fill in those gaps. Maybe you want a therapist, a support group, or to meet new mom friends. Check out the Resources on page 167 for more information.

Growth is painful, messy, and imperfect. In section 3, we spoke about grace and patience with yourself. As you complete this journal, take a moment to write down your commitment to yourself and how you will incorporate grace into that commitment. A commitment is often an affirmation of what is possible. For example, "I commit to being patient with myself and trusting in my process and believing that I am doing my best."

I am strong, capable, and imperfect, and I am committed to learning and growing!

A Final Word

Congratulations on getting to the end of this journal! Making it this far is a significant milestone. I encourage you to take what you need from this journal when you need it. Don't pressure yourself to do it all right now. Remember, taking small steps is still progress.

Continue getting to know yourself and understanding your experiences, reactions, and needs. Knowing those things and learning how to communicate them effectively will reduce much of the tension you may be experiencing within yourself, in relationship with your partner, and in interactions with your stepchildren.

Prioritize the relationship you have with your partner. You should present a united front to your children. It's important to connect intentionally. Keep conversations about the kids separate from everyday check-ins. It's easy to let conversations about the children account for much of what you talk about, but if that happens, the love and connection you two have for each other will be neglected.

That said, prioritize empathy and compassion toward the children as well. Children's behaviors are a sign of something; they indicate potential emotional needs or reactions to change. When talking with your children about behavior, focus first on what the underlying emotions or needs may be. Try to connect to those emotions with them, and focus on how they can express those things in a healthy way (see "Emotional Coaching," page 95).

Finally, connect with yourself and be mindful of how you process information. Create a filter for your thoughts by asking, *Is what I'm thinking gentle or harsh toward myself?* Take time for yourself away from the family and enjoy activities that are just for you. You may always feel guilty about it, but that doesn't mean you're doing something wrong. Sometimes those feelings are there because you're doing something new, and our brains don't react well to change.

Remember, change is hard, and it never looks perfect. Embrace the messiness of the experience and know that you can and will use this experience to become the best version of yourself. I'm so excited for you!

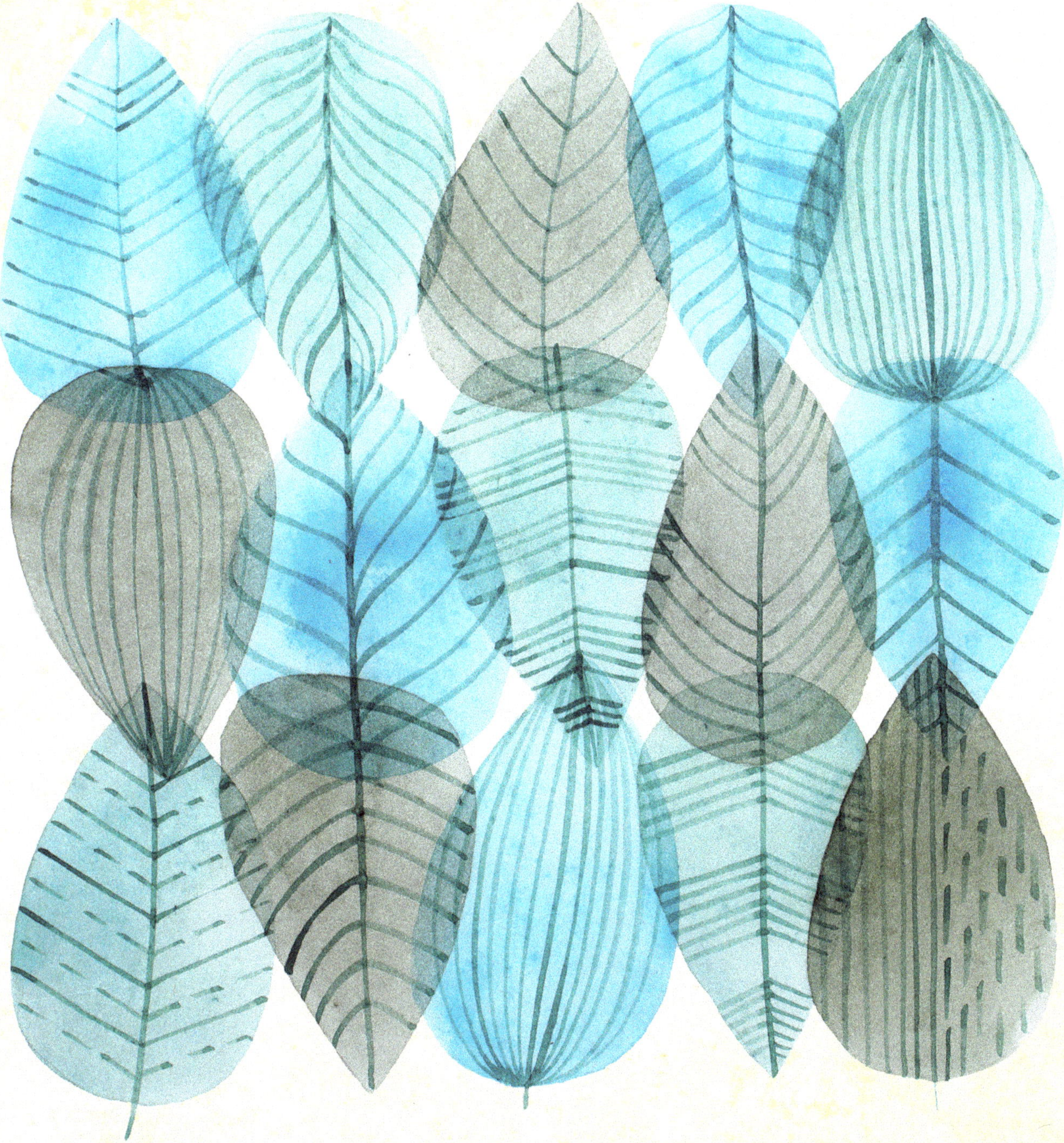

Resources

Finding a therapist or counselor in your area:
Psychology Today: PsychologyToday.com, You can use filters on this site to look for free groups and therapists with sliding-scale options. Your local YMCA, church, or community mental health agency will also offer free or reduced-fee options.

Stepfamily resources:
Gottman Card Deck app: Gottman.com/couples/apps, or available on your app store for free. Download this app for great tools and talking points to use with your partner!

National Stepfamily Resource Center: Stepfamilies.info. This website has a ton of great information and resources and creative ways to connect with others!

Blogs for stepmoms:
ThisLifeInProgress.com

Stepmomming.com

GradyBirdBlog.com

Online magazines for stepmoms:
StepMomMag.com

StepparentMagazine.com

Facebook groups:
Stepmomming Ain't Easy: Facebook.com/groups/stepmommingainteasy

Step-Mom Support: Facebook.com/stepmomsupportgroup

I'm a Stepmom . . . I'm Kind of a Big Deal: Facebook.com/groups/imastepmomimkindofabigdeal

References

Angelou, Maya. *Rainbow in the Cloud: The Wisdom and Spirit of Maya Angelou.* New York: Random House, 2014.

Branden, Nathaniel. *A Woman's Self-Esteem: Struggles and Triumphs in the Search for Identity.* San Francisco, CA: John Wiley & Sons, 2012.

Brown, Brené. "Brené Brown: 3 Ways to Set Boundaries." Oprah.com. https://www.oprah.com/spirit/how-to-set-boundaries-brene-browns-advice.

Brown, Brené. *Daring Greatly: How the Courage to Be Vulnerable Transforms the Way We Live, Love, Parent, and Lead.* New York: Avery, 2015.

Edelman, Marian Wright. "Kids First." *Mother Jones,* May/June 1991.

Gottman, John M., and Nan Silver. *The Seven Principles for Making Marriage Work: A Practical Guide from the Country's Foremost Relationship Expert.* 2nd ed. New York: Harmony Books, 2015.

Kong, Francis J. "Won't Be Easy but It Will Last." Blog, October 22, 2020. https://franciskong.com/blog/wont-be-easy-but-it-will-last/.

Lisa Olivera Therapy. "Setting Boundaries." https://lisaoliveratherapy.com/on-setting-boundaries.

Salinger, J. D. *The Catcher in the Rye.* New York: Back Bay Books, 2010.

Thomas, Iain S. *Every Word You Cannot Say.* Kansas City, MO: Andrews McMeel Publishing, 2019.

Winfrey, Oprah. "What Oprah Knows for Sure About Regaining Your Balance." Oprah.com, April 15, 2003. https://www.oprah.com/spirit/what-oprah-knows-for-sure-about-regaining-your-balance.

About the Author

SONYA JENSEN, LMFT, is a licensed marriage and family therapist, relationship coach, author, and speaker who seeks to inspire and educate couples with practical and relatable tools. A candid voice for relationship health, she brings her passion for relationship education to her podcast *@LoveandSexUnfiltered* and online at SonyaJensen.com. Find her on Instagram @thesonyajensen.

CPSIA information can be obtained
at www.ICGtesting.com
Printed in the USA
JSHW032113041021
19277JS00001B/3

9 781638 079040